Do you ever dream?
Stories are like dreams.
They can take you to
faraway places.

They can remind you of
good times. They can make
you feel happy and
warm inside.

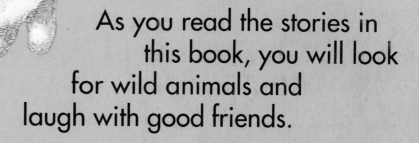

As you read the stories in
this book, you will look
for wild animals and
laugh with good friends.

Read on and dream
up your own stories
during this part of

HOUGHTON MIFFLIN
The Literature Experience
READING

Cover, Introduction, and Title Page Illustration by John Sandford.

Acknowledgments appear on page 126.

Printed in the U.S.A.

ISBN: 0-395-51915-2

DEFGHIJ-VH-9987654321

DREAM A STORY

Senior Author
John J. Pikulski

Senior Coordinating Author
J. David Cooper

Senior Consulting Author
William K. Durr

Coordinating Authors
Kathryn H. Au
M. Jean Greenlaw
Marjorie Y. Lipson
Susan Page
Sheila W. Valencia
Karen K. Wixson

Authors
Rosalinda B. Barrera
Ruth P. Bunyan
Jacqueline L. Chaparro
Jacqueline C. Comas
Alan N. Crawford
Robert L. Hillerich
Timothy G. Johnson
Jana M. Mason
Pamela A. Mason
William E. Nagy
Joseph S. Renzulli
Alfredo Schifini

Senior Advisor
Richard C. Anderson

Advisors
Christopher J. Baker
Charles Peters

HOUGHTON MIFFLIN COMPANY   BOSTON
Atlanta   Dallas   Geneva, Illinois   Palo Alto   Princeton   Toronto

3

8

WILD ANIMALS, COME OUT!

BOOK 1

12

Have You Seen the Crocodile?
by Colin West

32

I Caught a Fish
a traditional counting rhyme

47

Animal Homes
a photo essay

50

Sophie and Jack
by Judy Taylor

POETRY

43

Giraffes Don't Huff
by Karla Kuskin

44

One Little Elephant
*from a traditional counting rhyme
in English*

45

Un elefante se balanceaba
*from a traditional counting rhyme
in Spanish*

46

Lion
by Mary Ann Hoberman

READ ALONG BOOK

Monkeys in the Jungle
by Angie Sage

72

Good Friends, Good Times

BOOK 2

76

A Playhouse for Monster
by Virginia Mueller

94

Friends Around the World
a photo essay

96

The More We Get Together
a traditional song

109

Toby in the Country, Toby in the City
by Maxine Zohn Bozzo

POETRY

105

The New Girl

by Charlotte Zolotow

107

A New Friend

by Marjorie Allen Anderson

108

Best Friend

by William Wise

READ ALONG BOOK

I Need a Friend

by Sherry Kafka

BOOK 1

WILD ANIMALS, COME OUT!

If you met a wild animal, it just might hide from you! Where do you think it might go? The animals in these stories have some funny hiding places. Read about these animals and join them in a game of hide-and-seek.

Big Book

Monkeys in the Jungle
Angie Sage

The animals in this book live in many different places. They also like to hide! Can you guess where they are?

Read this book together to find out where the animals might be.

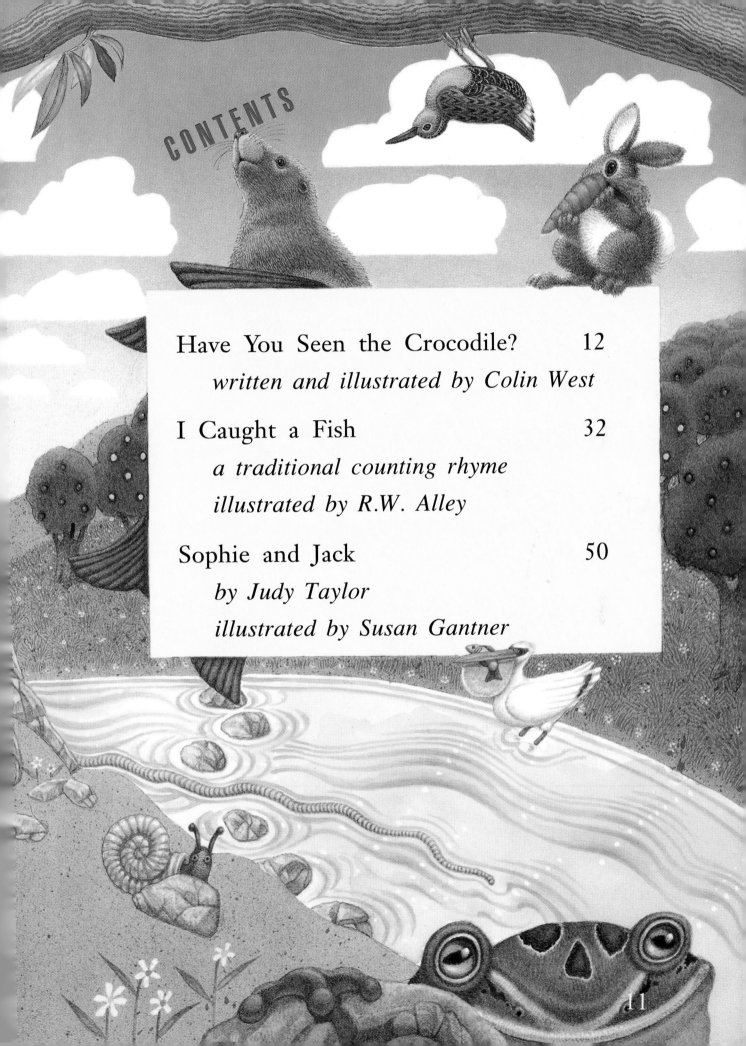

CONTENTS

Have You Seen the Crocodile?   12
written and illustrated by Colin West

I Caught a Fish   32
a traditional counting rhyme
illustrated by R.W. Alley

Sophie and Jack   50
by Judy Taylor
illustrated by Susan Gantner

HAVE YOU SEEN THE
CROCODILE?

Written and Illustrated by Colin West

"Have you seen the crocodile?"
asked the parrot.

"No," said the dragonfly.

"Have you seen the crocodile?"
asked the parrot
and the dragonfly.

"No,"
said the
bumble bee.

"Have you seen the crocodile?"
asked the parrot
and the dragonfly
and the bumble bee.

"No," said the butterfly.

"Have you seen the crocodile?"
asked the parrot
and the dragonfly
and the bumble bee
and the butterfly.

"No," said the hummingbird.

"Have you seen the crocodile?"
asked the parrot
and the dragonfly
and the bumble bee
and the butterfly
and the hummingbird.

"No," said the frog.

23

"No one's seen the crocodile!"
said the parrot
and the dragonfly
and the bumble bee
and the butterfly
and the hummingbird
and the frog.

"I'VE SEEN THE CROCODILE!" snapped the crocodile.

"But, has anyone seen the parrot
and the dragonfly
and the bumble bee
and the butterfly
and the hummingbird
and the frog?"

asked the crocodile.

Jungle Puppets

When the crocodile said, "I'VE SEEN THE CROCODILE," how do you think it sounded?

Make some puppets like the animals in the story. Then as you read the story aloud, put on a jungle puppet play! Make your animals sound just like the ones in the story.

Meet the Author and Illustrator
Colin West

When he was a little boy, Colin West practiced magic tricks. He also liked to read about plants and animals.

When he grew up, Mr. West went to art school. He has been writing and drawing pictures for storybooks ever since. He also writes poetry.

I Caught a Fish

a traditional counting rhyme

illustrated by R.W. Alley

One, two, three, four, five,
Once I caught a fish alive,

Six, seven, eight, nine, ten,
Then I let it go again.

One, two, three, four, five,
Once I caught a bird alive,

Six, seven, eight, nine, ten,
Then I let it go again.

One, two, three, four, five,
Once I caught a monkey alive,

Six, seven, eight, nine, ten,
Then I let it go again.

One, two, three, four, five,
Once I caught a giraffe alive,

Six, seven, eight, nine, ten,
Then I let it go again.

One, two, three, four, five,
Once I caught a LION alive,

Six, seven, eight, nine, ten,
Then I let it go again!

Add a Verse

You read about five different animals in this funny counting rhyme. Now try making up a new verse.

Think of another wild animal and tell about it in your rhyme. Then draw a picture to go with it. You'll be ready to teach the class your new verse!

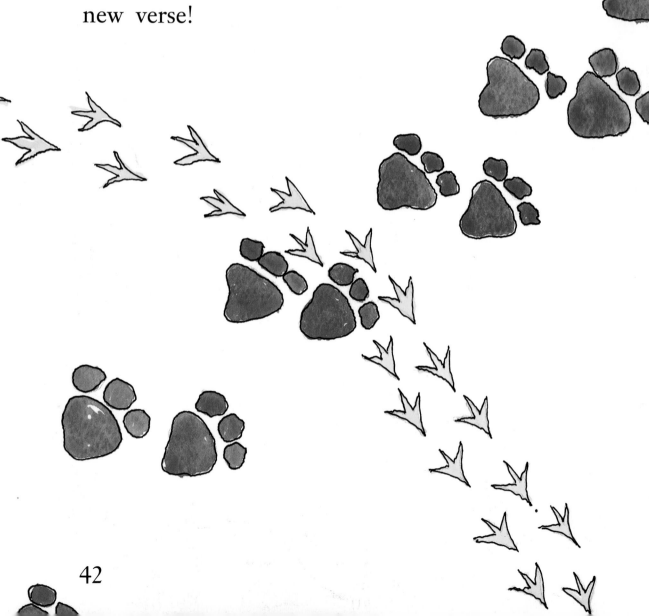

Giraffes Don't Huff

Giraffes don't huff or hoot or howl
They never grump, they never growl
They never roar, they never riot,
They eat green leaves
And just keep quiet.

by Karla Kuskin

One Little Elephant
from a traditional counting rhyme in English

One little elephant,
Out for a run,
Climbed up a spider's web
Just for fun.
He tiptoed across,
He did a little dance,
And then he called down
For some *more* ele–phants.

Two little elephants,
Out for a run . . .

Three little elephants . . .

Un elefante se balanceaba

from a traditional counting rhyme in Spanish

Un elefante
se balanceaba
sobre la tela
de una araña,
como veía
que resistía
fue a llamar
a otro elefante.

Dos elefantes
se balanceaban ...

Tres elefantes ...

45

Lion

Look!
A lion!
Mighty beast.
   (Might he
   Bite me
   For a feast?)
Though I know
He wouldn't dare,
   I'm mighty glad

                     he's over there.

by Mary Ann Hoberman

ANIMAL HOMES

Wild animals look for safe places to make their homes. Do you think the animals in these pictures found good homes?

prairie dog

robins

rainbow fish

black-legged kittiwakes

clownfish

rabbit

bald eagle

raccoon

wolf pups

49

50

SOPHIE & JACK

by Judy Taylor

illustrated by Susan Gantner

It was a wonderful day for a picnic.

Everyone was hungry.

Soon there was not much left.

"Let's play hide-and-seek," said Sophie.

"I'll hide," said Jack.

"I'll seek," said Sophie.

Jack hid behind a tree with his eyes shut tight.

Sophie shut her eyes, too, and counted to ten.

Sophie found Jack very quickly.

"Now me," she said.

Jack turned his back and counted to ten.

Sophie hid in the grass with her eyes
shut tight.

Jack found her very quickly.

"Me again," said Jack, and he ran off
to hide.

Sophie couldn't find Jack anywhere.

Can you?

Where's Sophie?

It's Sophie's turn to hide again. Can you think of a good hiding place for her — a place where Jack won't find her?

Draw a picture of Sophie's new hiding place and write a sentence about it.

Meet the Author
Judy Taylor

Judy Taylor used to help other authors write books. She did such a good job that the Queen of England gave her a prize!

Now Mrs. Taylor writes her own books. She began with *Sophie and Jack.* Later on, she also wrote some storybooks about a mouse named Dudley.

Meet the Illustrator
Susan Gantner

Susan Gantner's drawings can be seen in museums. She first drew pictures of hippos for greeting cards. Then she began to draw pictures for Judy Taylor's books. After that, her two hippos became known as Sophie and Jack.

MORE WILD ANIMALS

Monkeys in the Jungle
by Angie Sage

You know where the monkeys live. Now read the book again. Can you remember where all the other animals live?

Junglewalk
by Nancy Tafuri

A young boy reads a book about jungle animals. Then he falls asleep and meets them in a wonderful dream.

We Hide, You Seek

by Jose Aruego and Ariane Dewey
A rhinoceros wants to play
hide-and-seek with its friends.
Read about all the good hiding places
they find!

Animals Sleeping

by Masayuki Yabuuchi
Did you know that
flamingos sleep standing
up — on just one leg? This
book is full of surprises about
how animals sleep!

"Pardon?" Said the Giraffe

by Colin West
A frog wonders what it's
like to be tall, like Giraffe.
Then Frog takes a ride on
Giraffe's nose — and gets a
surprise!

BOOK 2

Good Friends, Good Times

What is more fun than doing something you like? Doing something you like with a friend!

Read these stories and poems about friends. Then read them with one of *your* friends, and share some good times.

Big Book

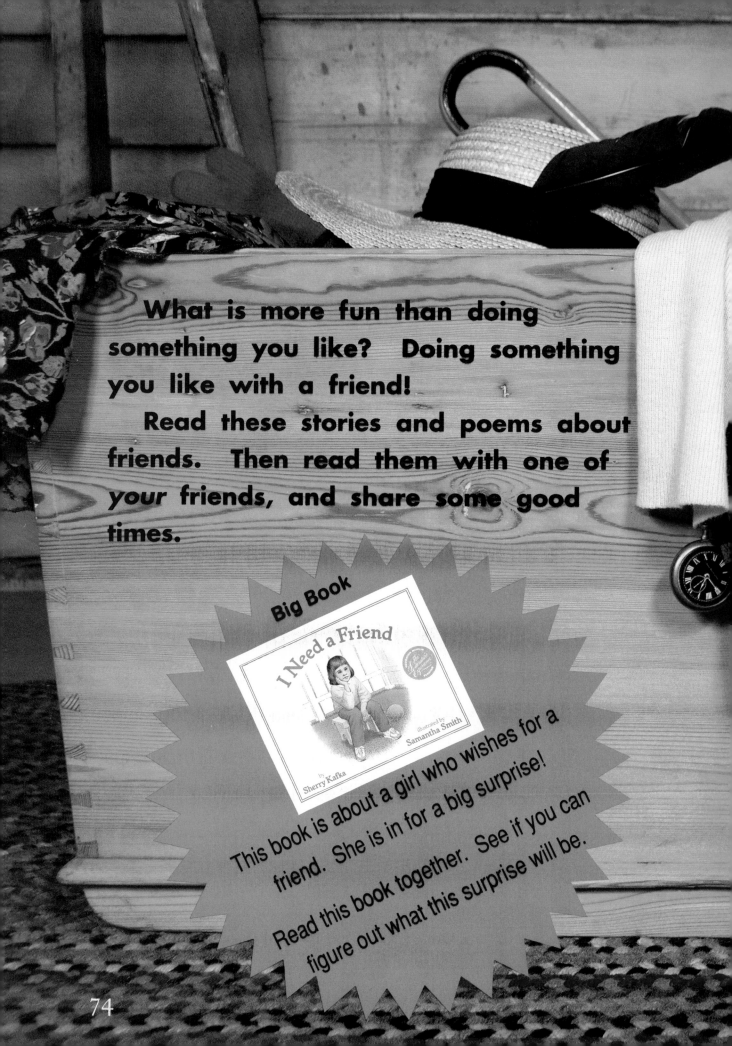

This book is about a girl who wishes for a friend. She is in for a big surprise! Read this book together. See if you can figure out what this surprise will be.

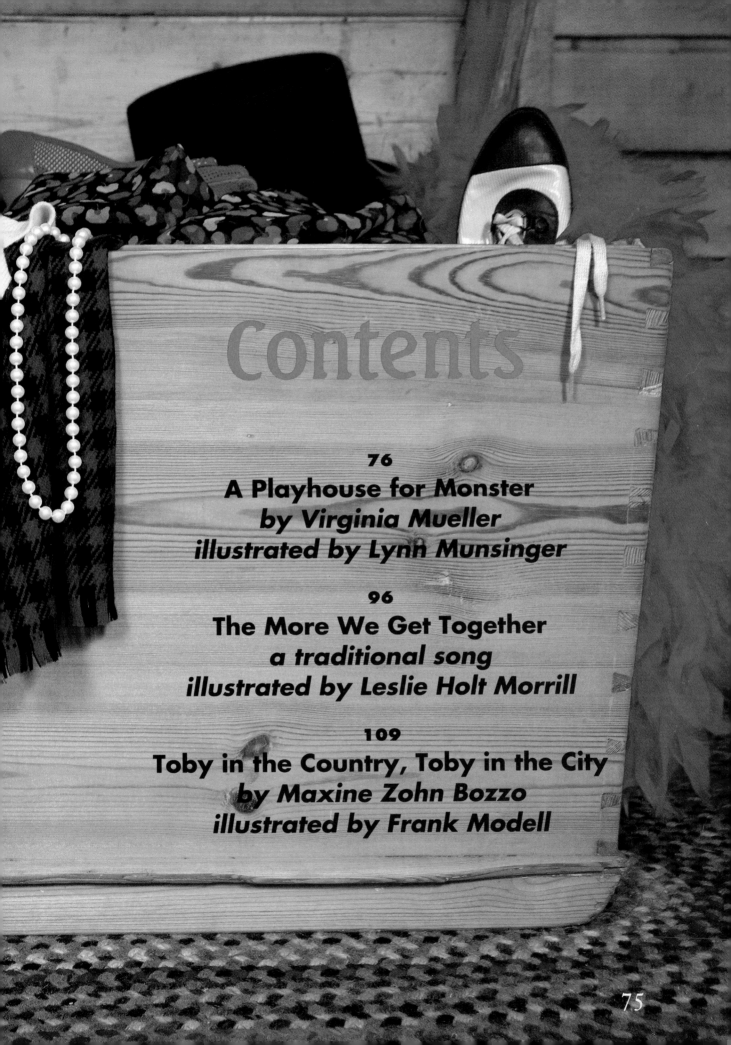

Contents

76

A Playhouse for Monster
by Virginia Mueller
illustrated by Lynn Munsinger

96

The More We Get Together
a traditional song
illustrated by Leslie Holt Morrill

109

Toby in the Country, Toby in the City
by Maxine Zohn Bozzo
illustrated by Frank Modell

A PLAYHOUSE FOR MONSTER

by Virginia Mueller

illustrated by Lynn Munsinger

Monster made a sign. It said KEEP OUT!

"This is *my* playhouse," Monster said.

"These are *my* walls."

"*My* roof."

"*My* windows."

"*My* door."

"*My* chair."

"*My* table."

"*My* cookie."

"*My* glass of milk."

But Monster wasn't happy.

"I know," he said.
"I need *two* chairs."

"*Two* cookies."

"*Two* glasses of milk."

Monster made a new sign.
It said WELCOME!

Make Posters, Make Friends!

Monster made a new sign for the playhouse. It said "Welcome." Can you think of some good ways to make a friend feel welcome?

Make a poster about one of your ideas. You could roll up your poster and put a ribbon around it. Then you could give it to a special friend!

Meet the Author

When Virginia Mueller was a little girl, she liked to read poetry. Her first poem was published when she was only ten years old! Since then, Mrs. Mueller has written more than fifteen storybooks.

Meet the Illustrator

Lynn Munsinger draws many kinds of pictures, but most of all she likes to draw monsters. She doesn't like scary ones. She likes to draw the funny kind — like Monster and his friend!

Friends Around the World

ITALY

SPAIN

RUSSIA

KENYA

CHINA

CANADA

CZECHOSLOVAKIA

ECUADOR

BHUTAN

95

THE MORE WE

illustrated by
Leslie Holt Morrill

The more we get together,
Together, together,
The more we get together,
The happier we'll be.

96

GET TOGETHER

Your friends are my friends,
And my friends are your friends.
The more we get together,
The happier we'll be.

STREET
FAIR

SATURDAY
9:30-5:30

97

The more we play together,
Together, together,
The more we play together,
The happier we'll be.

The more we laugh together,
Together, together,
The more we laugh together,
The happier we'll be.

99

The more we sing together,
Together, together,
The more we sing together,
The happier we'll be.

The more we dance together,
Together, together,
The more we dance together,
The happier we'll be.

The more we get together,
Together, together,
The more we get together,
The happier we'll be.

Your friends are my friends,
And my friends are your friends.
The more we get together,
The happier we'll be.

LET'S SING TOGETHER

Make up a new verse for this song. Think of something you like to do with your friends. Add a new word to the song to tell about it.

Act out your word first — don't sing it. See if your friends can guess what it is. Then sing your new verse together.

The more we skate together,
Together, together,
The more we skate together,
The happier we'll be!

Poems About Friends

The New Girl

I can feel
we're much the same,
though I don't
know your name.

What friends
we're going to be
when I know you
and you know me!

by Charlotte Zolotow

A New Friend

They've taken in the furniture;
I watched them carefully.
I wondered, "Will there be a child
Just right to play with me?"

So I peeked through the garden fence
(I couldn't wait to see.)
I found the little boy next door
Was peeking back at me.

by Marjorie Allen Anderson

Best Friend

I've got a best friend.
She is funny and clever.
She will stay my best friend
For ever and ever.

by William Wise

TOBY IN THE COUNTRY,

TOBY IN THE CITY

by Maxine Zohn Bozzo ● *illustrated by Frank Modell*

I live in the country, and my name is Toby.

I live in the city, and my name is Toby.

My house looks like this.

My house looks like this.

My street looks like this, and has trees.

My street looks like this, and has trees.

I go to school with my sister and brother.

I go to school with my sister and brother.

After school I like to play with my friends.

After school I like to play with my friends.

Sometimes it's winter in the country . . .
and I like to play in the snow.

Sometimes it's winter in the city . . .
and I like to play in the snow.

When it is spring in the country...
I see lots of flowers.

When it is spring in the city...
I see lots of flowers.

When summer comes to the country . . .
I like to go to the beach.

When summer comes to the city . . .
I like to go to the beach.

Sometimes when it is fall in the country . . .
I like to play in the leaves.

Sometimes when it is fall in the city . . .
I like to play in the leaves.

I like to live in the country.

I like to live in the city.

I like to visit the city.

I like to visit the country.

And I LIKE YOU!

A BOOK ABOUT YOU

You have learned some things about the country Toby and the city Toby. Now make a book about *you*. Tell about yourself and where you live. Then let your friends read all about you.

Meet the Author

Maxine Bozzo grew up in New York City. She spends most of her time writing. Ms. Bozzo also helps artists sell their work, and she makes jewelry out of beads. Ms. Bozzo is married to an artist. They have three children.

Meet the Illustrator

Frank Modell was drawing cartoons before he was in kindergarten! When he grew up, Mr. Modell wrote and illustrated storybooks and did some art work for the *Sesame Street* and *The Electric Company* TV shows.

Today Mr. Modell draws cartoons for a magazine.

Drawing by Modell, (c) 1983
The New Yorker Magazine, Inc.

124

Meet More Friends

I Need a Friend *by Sherry Kafka*

Together you read about the two new friends in this book. Now read it again — to one of *your* friends!

Going for a Walk

by Beatrice Schenk de Regniers

A girl meets many animals on her walk. Then she finds a friend. Who do you think it will be?

A Country Far Away *by Nigel Gray*

Do you like to read about places far away? Then you'll love this book about two boys from different countries. You'll be surprised at how alike they are!

I Have a Friend *by Keiko Narahashi*

A boy tells about a special friend who follows him everywhere. You have a friend like this, too!

Acknowledgments

For each of the selections listed below, grateful acknowledgment is made for permission to excerpt and/or reprint original or copyrighted material, as follows:

Major Selections

Have You Seen the Crocodile? by Colin West (J. B. Lippincott). Copyright © 1986 by Colin West. Reprinted by permission of Harper and Row, Publishers, Inc.

A Playhouse for Monster, text copyright © 1985 by Virginia Mueller. Illustrations copyright © 1985 by Lynn Munsinger. Originally published in hardcover by Albert Whitman and Company. All rights reserved. Used with permission.

Sophie and Jack, text copyright © 1982 by Judy Taylor, illustrations copyright © 1982 by Susan Gantner. Reprinted by permission of Philomel Books, and The Bodley Head.

Toby in the Country, Toby in the City, by Maxine Zohn Bozzo, illustrated by Frank Modell. Text copyright © 1982 by Maxine Zohn Bozzo. Illustrations copyright © 1982 by Frank Modell. Reprinted by permission of Greenwillow Books, a division of William Morrow and Co., Inc.

Poetry

"Best Friend," from *All On A Summer's Day* by William Wise. Copyright © 1971 by William Wise. Reprinted by permission.

"Giraffes Don't Huff," from *Roar and More* by Karla Kuskin. Copyright © 1956 by Karla Kuskin. Reprinted by permission of HarperCollins Publisners.

"Lion," from *The Raucous Auk* by Mary Ann Hoberman. Text copyright © 1973 by Mary Ann Hoberman. Reprinted by permission of the Gina Maccoby Literary Agency.

"A New Friend," by Marjorie Allen Anderson. Used by permission of *Highlights for Children*, Columbus, OH. Copyright © 1950.

"The New Girl," from *Everything Glistens and Everything Sings* by Charlotte Zolotow. Copyright © 1987 by Charlotte Zolotow. Reprinted by permission of Harcourt Brace Jovanovich, Inc.

Others

Cartoon by Frank Modell from *The New Yorker Cartoon Album 1975–1985*. Copyright © 1975–1985. Reprinted by permission.

Read Along Books

The Read Along Books shown on pages 10, 70, 74, and 124 are available from Houghton Mifflin Company and are reprinted with permission from various publishers. Jacket artists for these books are listed below.

I Need a Friend, by Sherry Kafka. Jacket art by Samantha Smith, copyright © 1991 by Houghton Mifflin Company.

Monkeys in the Jungle, by Angie Sage. Jacket art by Angie Sage, copyright © 1989 by Angie Sage.

Additional Recommended Reading

Houghton Mifflin Company wishes to thank the following publishers for permission to reproduce their book covers on pages 70, 71, 124 and 125.

Greenwillow Books, a division of William Morrow & Company, Inc.:
We Hide, You Seek, by Jose Aruego and Ariane Dewey. Jacket art by Jose Aruego and Ariane Dewey, copyright © 1979 by Jose Aruego and Ariane Dewey.

Harper & Row, Publishers, Inc.:
Going for a Walk, by Beatrice Schenk de Regniers. Jacket art by Beatrice Schenk de Regniers, copyright © 1961 by Beatrice Schenk de Regniers.

Margaret K. McElderry Books, an imprint of Macmillan Publishing Company:
I Have a Friend, by Keiko Narahashi. Jacket art by Keiko Narahashi, copyright © 1987 by Keiko Narahashi.

Orchard Books, a division of Franklin Watts, Inc. and Andersen Press Ltd.:
A Country Far Away, by Nigel Gray. Jacket art by Philippe Dupasquier, copyright © 1988 by Philippe Dupasquier. First published in Great Britain by Andersen Press Limited.

Credits

Program design Carbone Smolan Associates

Cover design Carbone Smolan Associates

Design **8–71** Liska & Associates, Inc.; **72–125** Imprint

Illustrations **8–11** John Sandford; **12–29** Colin West; **30** Chris Froeter; **31** Colin West; **32–41** R.W. Alley; **42** Chris Froeter; **43** Linda Cornell; **44–45** Diane Jaquith; **46** Linda Cornell; **50–69** Susan Gantner; **70–71** John Sandford; **76–91** Lynn Munsinger; **93** Susan Jaekel; **94–95** Linda Phinney **96–104** Leslie Holt Morrill; **105** Catharine O'Neill; **106–107** Susan Swan; **108** Gail Owens; **109–121** Frank Modell; **122** Catharine O'Neill; **123** Susan Jaekel

Photography **47** (center) Animals Animals/© Richard Kolar, (right) Animals Animals/© M. Austerman, (bottom) Jeff Rotman; **48** (top) Superstock, (center) Jeff Rotman, (bottom) Animals Animals; **48–49** Leonard Lee Rue III/ Superstock; **49** (top) Animals Animals/© Ray Richardson, (bottom) Animals Animals/© Mark Stouffer; **72–75** Elliott Smith; **92** Alec Duncan; **93** (top) Nancy Pieper, The Sheboygan Press; **93** (bottom) Courtesy of Lynn Munsinger; **94** (top) TSW-CLICK/Chicago Ltd., (center right) Bruce Davidson/Magnum, (center left) David Ball/The Stock Market, © (bottom) Paul Conklin/Uniphoto; **95** (top right) David Falconer/Frazier Library, (top left) P. & G. Bowater/The Image Bank, (center right) Karen Rantzman, (center left) Eastcott/Momatiuk/Woodfin Camp and Associates, (bottom) © Susan Katz; **123** (top) courtesy of Maxine Bozzo, (bottom) Anne Hall; **Back cover** Courtesy of Julia MacRae Books, a division of Walker Books Limited